POKER

Written by meme design

TOP THAT!™

CONTENTS

GUTS POKER

These games are based on one very simple principle. The cards are dealt, and players must decide if they are "in" or "out." If a player calls "out," they fold, and the best hand of the players who have called 'in' wins. The other players who called "in" but did not win, must match the amount of money in the pot.

If only one player calls "in," they automatically win the pot. Guts can be expensive game to play but if luck is on your side, you can also win big.

Players can agree to cap the pot which then limits how much one player can win or lose in a single hand. If a limit is set this will mean that if the pot exceeds this limit, the winner will only take the agreed amount and each loser will only pay the same.

BASIC GUTS GAME

Players	*3-20*
Cards	*A standard 52-card deck*
Initial deal	*Two cards to each player*
Winner	*Highest hand*

The dealer deals two cards face down to each player. If the cards are the same, the player has a pair. If not, the high card rule applies.

In or out?

Everyone in turn says whether they are in or out. The "ins" ante up while the players who have called "out" have no further interest in the pot. This allows players to base their decision on the actions of other players. (See the variation Coin declare on page 110 for a neat way around this.)

The player with the highest hand of those who nominated to be in, wins the pot. The other players who were still in the hand then have to match the amount that was in the pot to form the kitty for the next round. For example, if a player wins the pot and it is $1, the three other players must all put in $1 each to make the new pot. This will make the new pot $3.

Variations

The kitty—Two extra hands are dealt as a blind hand in the center of the table. These are not revealed until the showdown. All players still in the game at the showdown must not only beat each other but the hand in the middle as well. If the kitty has the best hand, then everyone pays the pot! If everyone in the game calls "out," then the dealer wins by default, and would only need to call "in" to win the pot. This way, the dealer must still beat the kitty.

Coin declare—The normal format for play is that calling "in" or "out" goes round the table starting with the player to the left of the dealer, and ending with the dealer. Coin declare allows all players to declare "in" or "out" simultaneously. Players put both hands and a coin (or counter) under the table. When the dealer says to, all players open up one hand over the table, either holding the coin if they are in, or revealing an empty hand if they are out.

ETIQUETTE

It's fine to take your time but excessively slow play can annoy other players. It might seem like a good idea to psyche out the opposition by making them wait but it's better to just play well and win!

GUTS FOR WIMPS

Players	*3-20*
Cards	*A standard 52-card deck*
Initial deal	*Two cards to each player*
Winner	*Highest hand*

This is played as per the basic guts game but if all the players decide to go "out" all reveal their hands. The player with the highest hand must pay a specified amount into the pot for the next round instead of all the players re-anteing for a new hand.

INDIAN GUTS

Players	*Up to 52 players*
Cards	*A standard 52-card deck*
Initial deal	*One card to each player*
Winner	*Highest card*

One card is dealt to each player. Players hold their card face out against their forehead. The dealer asks everyone if they are "in" or "out". Those remaining "in" show their cards. Highest card wins! This game can be played with two cards.

BID POKER

The main feature of bid poker is that the cards are auctioned off one at a time. Players bid on cards as they are dealt and put the money into the pot.

STANDARD BID POKER

Players	*3-8*
Cards	*A standard 52-card deck*
Initial deal	*Five cards to each player, face down*
Winner	*Highest hand*

All players ante, then each is dealt five cards face down, which they may look at. One card is turned face up in the middle. Each player in turn, starting with the player on the left of the dealer, has the option to bid for the card. Each subsequent bid must be higher than the previous, or the player can pass. Once a player passes, they can have no further interest in that card, but can bid on future cards.

Once everyone has passed except for one player, that player puts their bid in the pot and adds the card to their hand. A card from their hand is then discarded, and the dealer flips over the next card from the deck for auction.

The player to the left of whoever started the bidding previously, starts the round of bidding for the next card. Play proceeds until everyone has started the bidding once, then there is the showdown. Best hand wins.

Variation

Bid Slam—In this variation, instead of discarding the chosen card to a discard pile, the player who bought the last card slams (gives the card to) the person of their choice. They, in turn, choose a card and place it face down in front of another player. Before looking at the card, this player has to discard one card, then pick up the card they have been given.

POKER TALK

Don't sound like it's your first time at the table. Talk like a pro using these poker phrases.

Throwing a party—Several less experienced players contributing large bets to the pot.

A Dolly Parton—A straight using the cards 5, 6, 7, 8, and 9 (nine to five!)

Cranberry—A player who consistently calls against the pot odds.

Ducks—Two 2s is a pair of ducks.

CASINO POKER

Poker games played in casinos vary dramatically, from the very popular Caribbean stud, which looks quite familiar, to the ancient Chinese tile game pai gow. There are also poker games that can be played on "poker machines" or "video machines," which are often linked to progressive jackpots, so if you win, you can win big!

CARIBBEAN STUD POKER

This game became a favorite on Caribbean cruise ships, hence the name. Unlike traditional poker, where you are competing against the other players at the table, here you only have to beat the dealer.

Once you place your ante in the designated square, you are dealt your five-card hand, face down. Often the ante will be a substantial amount, unlike a nominal donation when you play at home. The dealer receives their hand of four cards face down plus one card face up. Players may look at their hand, but must not share information with each other. Once you look at your cards, you must decide if you are going to bet or fold. If you decide to bet, the amount will usually be twice your ante and this will be placed in the betting box. If you fold, the dealer will collect your cards to be discarded and you will lose your ante. Betting and discarding is carried out as per standard stud rules.

Once all of the bets are placed, the dealer shows all of their cards. The game will only continue if the dealer's hand qualifies, which means that it must contain an ace or a king, or better. If the dealer's hand does not qualify, the player's ante is paid even money and the bet is withdrawn.

If the dealer qualifies, each player's hand is compared to that of the dealer and the best hand wins. Of course, if the dealer's hand is better, the ante and bet are lost. When the player wins, both the ante and the bet are paid. Payouts are determined by the rank of each hand, and these will be displayed clearly near the table. If the dealer and player's hand tie, the ante and bet are returned to the player.

Some tables will also be linked to a progressive jackpot, where you have the opportunity to win a substantial amount of money if you hold a particular hand, like a royal flush.

GAME TIP

Most new players lose money by playing too many starting hands. Professional and other top players generally only play twenty to thirty percent of their starting hands. Save your money for higher value hands to help limit the element of luck in your play.

PAI GOW POKER

This poker variant is the card version of the very popular ancient Chinese game of pai gow, which is played with special tiles similar to dominoes. The goal of the ancient game was to "make nine," which is what pai gow means.

The game is played with a 52-card deck and one joker. Each player must make two poker hands both ranking higher than the dealer's two poker hands. Each player receives seven cards, and they must be split into a high hand consisting of five cards, and a low hand consisting of two cards. The joker can only be used as an ace or to complete a straight, a flush or a straight flush.

The ranking of hands follows traditional poker rankings, therefore, a royal flush is the highest hand and two aces is the best-ranking low hand.

A player may opt to be the bank, in which case that they must pay the other players on winning hands, but collect the losing hands for themselves. The casino will often tax winnings at a predetermined percentage. If no player nominates to be the bank, the casino will bank all the bets. No player can be the bank for every hand. Even if a player is banking the table, the casino dealer still plays.

Before the deal of the cards, three dice are rolled and the results determine the order of the deal. Each player is then dealt their seven cards from which to make two hands. The rank of the high hand must be higher than the rank of the low hand.

The casino dealer must set their hand according to a fixed set of game rules. Where the low and high hands are the same the bank wins all ties.

It is good to remember that because you need to win both hands, you must split your best cards between the two hands. For example, if you were dealt four aces and a joker, rather than making five of a kind in the high hand, it may be better to use two in the low hand (an unbeatable hand), and leave the three of a kind in the high hand (which is still a very strong hand).

The betting, odds and payouts for pai gow poker are very complex and the rules can be different in each casino. It is advisable to look at these before starting to play.

GLOSSARY

Poker has its own terminology, which can be confusing to the
novice player. This comprehensive guide to the terms used in
this book should help you.

Ante

A small bet that is contributed to the
pot by each player at the beginning
of each new hand. This needs to be
paid before the cards are dealt.
Some games like Texas hold 'em use
blinds instead of an ante as an
initial payment to the pot.

Bet

To add money to the pot. This is
required at various times to stay in
the round and the game.

Blind bet

A forced bet that is paid by one or
more players before cards are dealt.
Blinds are normally paid by the two
players to the left of the dealer to
boost the money in the pot in hold

'em games. There are often two
blinds, the small and the large blind.

Bluff

This is often a tactic used when you
have a weak hand to try to get other
players to fold. A bluffing player
often has little or no chance of
actually winning a showdown.

Button

Usually a plastic disc, used to mark
a particular position at the table.

Call

This is when you match the current
bet. For example, if there was an
original bet of $5 by one player, and
then another raised it $5, you would
need to bet $10 to stay in the game.

Check

This is the equivalent of betting a zero.

Door Card

A door card is dealt face up.

Fold

This is when you discard your hand. It is usually done when you are not confident that you are going to win, or if someone is betting stakes you can't match.

Hand

A hand refers either to the round (everything that happens between shuffles) or to the individual player's cards.

Hole Card

Hole or "in the hole" is the name for cards which are dealt face down and are not revealed until later in the game.

House

The establishment running the game. This can be either the dealer in a friendly game at home, a poker house, or a casino.

Kicker

The highest card in a hand that is not used to form the poker hand. For example, if your hand is 7-7-9-Q-A, then the ace is the kicker. This can be an important card particularly when two players have the same pair.

Natural Hand

This is a hand that does not use any wild cards or jokers. In many games a natural hand the same rank as a hand using wild cards will be considered the winning hand.

Odds

Mathematical equation used to determine the likelihood of something happening. The odds of poker look at the chances of you being dealt a hand, and beating the other players.

Pot

All the money in the middle of the poker table that goes to the winner of the hand.

Raise

When a player has opened a betting round, you need to bet more to increase the stakes.

Rank

This is the value or number of the card. There are thirteen ranks in a 52-card deck.

Showdown

This is the last stage of a game when the winner is determined. All players who have not folded during the game reveal their hands. If everyone folds, there is no showdown. Similarly, if there is only one player left, they are not required to show their cards.

Wild Card

A card that can be used as any other card to make a winning hand. For example, if you had A-A-7-7-W, you would say that the wild card was an ace so that you had a full house.

CONCLUSION

From this brief introduction you will probably have realized that, despite looking relatively simple on the surface, poker is a game of hidden depths and challenges.

It may look like a basic game of chance but many people have dedicated their lives to learning its intricacies. Professional poker is a big-money, high-stakes business and in the end it is mostly the casinos that win.

While it can take a lifetime to feel confident that you have mastered poker, you can have many hours of fun along the way. Remember though, that gambling can be addictive. The best way to avoid this is to concentrate on the social aspects of poker rather than the money-winning opportunities.

INTRODUCTION

Poker is a game of chance, skill, and psychology. With such a colorful history, it is no wonder that it has developed into one of the world's most popular card games, played both at home with friends, and in casinos. There are many different types of poker with even more variations for each game. Draw, stud, and shared games are the most commonly played.

POKER ELEMENTS

Although it is easier to win if you have a high hand, it does not mean that you will. If you have a good bluffing face and nerves of steel, you can win with a hand that's considerably lower than those of other players.

Professional players often use poker jargon, some of which has been used in this book. All the terms can be found in the glossary on pages 124-126.

This book is merely a guide to the rules of poker, with examples of different games. It is not meant to be used as a point of reference for tactics to employ when betting high stakes.

A word of warning. Please be aware that gambling can be addictive and may lead to many personal problems including debt. If you think you have a problem, please contact the Gamblers Anonymous association in your area.

All games, whether played in private or in a licensed venue, are entered into at your own risk, so it is worth remembering the adage of only betting what you can afford to lose.

HISTORY

The origin of poker is widely disputed. There are as many possible beginnings as there are variations of the game.

IN THE BEGINNING

It is widely believed that poker is a spin-off from Chinese dominoes, and was first played in China around AD 900. Another theory, recorded around the seventeenth century, places its origin with the Persian game "as nas," which requires a deck of 25 special cards with five suits. There are also links to "poque," which was played by the French when they colonized New Orleans around 1718. This game involved betting and bluffing and is believed to be the first use of a deck of cards containing the four suits we know today: hearts, diamonds, clubs, and spades.

Narrowing down the origin seems to be as difficult as landing a royal flush. However, it is most likely that poker derived its present-day rules from elements of many different games. In 1834, Jonathan H. Green wrote about the rules of a game that was being played on Mississippi riverboats, called the "cheating game." This was possibly the first written reference to the game he chose to call poker. He described a game played with two to four people, being dealt five cards each from a deck of twenty cards, using only the aces, kings, queens, jacks, and 10s.

RISING POPULARITY

By the time Green had written about poker it had become even more popular than three-card monte. Three-card monte had been the most common gambling game, however, it had a reputation for being rigged and often games were run by crooks.

Three-card monte appeared to be a simple game where the dealer had three cards that were placed face down and the players bet on which card they thought was the queen. If by chance punters bet on the correct card, diversionary tactics and muscle men were used to ensure that no money was ever paid out.

Poker was viewed as a more legitimate game because players were dealt their own hand and could determine their own fate.

QUOTES AND QUIPS

"There are few things that are so unpardonably neglected in our country as poker. The upper class knows very little about poker. Now and then you find ambassadors who have sort of a general knowledge of poker, but the ignorance of the people is fearful. Why, I have known clergymen, good men, kind-hearted, liberal, sincere, and all that, who did not know the meaning of a 'flush'. It is enough to make one ashamed of the species."

Mark Twain

In the early days of poker, the game was synonymous with cheating. This image has since been strengthened by the role that poker often plays in Western movies. Throughout most of the twentieth century poker did indeed inhabit a gray world of card sharks and professional gamblers, but as with most games and sports where big money becomes involved, the game has begun to come out of the shadows and into the limelight.

Gambling is now regarded as a mainstream leisure activity and as such is enjoyed by people all over the world. In the highly regulated world of the casinos, poker plays an integral part—but these days cheating is not only bad form, but bad for business too.

QUOTES AND QUIPS

"Is it a reasonable thing, I ask you, for a grown man to run about and hit a ball? Poker's the only game fit for a grown man. Then, your poker hand is against every man's, and every man's is against yours. Teamwork? Who ever made a fortune by teamwork? There's only one way to make a fortune, and that's to down the fellow who's up against you in poker."

Somerset Maugham

THE BASICS

Poker is generally played with a standard deck of 52 cards. Some variations of the game use multiple packs or jokers. The deck contains four suits: hearts, diamonds, spades and clubs, and generally, no suit is considered higher than another. The cards are ranked ace, king, queen, jack, 10, 9, 8, 7, 6, 5, 4, 3, 2, ace —the ace ranking high or low at the player's or house's choice.

ORDER OF PLAY

This is the basic order of play for many poker games.

1. All of the players are seated and the rules of the game are agreed. This would include betting limits, variations, and wild cards if any.

2. The ante (initial payment or bet) is paid to the pot by each player.

3. The cards are dealt, starting with the player immediately to the left of the dealer. These are dealt either face down or face up, depending on the game.

4. In games when players are able to look at their cards, they do so now.

5. In the first round of betting players take it in turn, starting from the player immediately to the left of the dealer, to either bet or fold.

6. In most games, after the first betting round, players may be dealt more cards, or cards previously dealt will be revealed.

7. In the subsequent rounds of betting, players may call, bet, or fold.

8. Different games have various numbers of betting rounds and ways that players receive new cards; sometimes cards are revealed that players have the option to include in their hand.

9. In most games there is a final betting round before the showdown.

10. All players remaining in the hand at the end will reveal their cards in the showdown. This is where the winner is established and the pot is won. If only one player remains they win the pot without disclosing their hand. If they have bluffed successfully throughout the game, they could, in fact, be holding low-ranking cards.

QUOTES AND QUIPS

"If, after the first twenty minutes, you don't know who the sucker at the poker table is, it's you."

Anon

Most games of poker are won by the highest hand. Here is a basic description of the hands, but a more detailed explanation is given on pages 20-27. The hands are ranked as follows (from high to low):

Five of a Kind
Only possible in games that include jokers or wild cards (W-K-K-K-K).

Royal Flush
A-K-Q-J-10, all of the same suit.

Straight Flush
Any sequence of five cards of the same suit (7-8-9-10-J).

Four of a Kind
Four cards of the same rank (K-K-K-K-3).

Full House
Three of a kind, plus any pair of the same rank (K-K-K-10-10).

Flush
Any five cards of the same suit, but not in sequence.

Straight
Five cards in sequence, but not in the same suit.

Three of a Kind
Three cards of the same rank, and two unpaired cards. Also known as trips (K-K-K-2-5).

Two Pair
Two different pairs (K-K-5-5-2).

Pair
Two cards of the same rank (Q-Q-8-4-A).

Highest Card
If no other hands are possible, the highest card in the hand. The high card rule applies to most poker games. When hands tie, for example, two players both have a pair of jacks, then the player with the highest card outside the pair wins.

WILD CARDS

Some games have wild cards. In some versions these wild cards take on whatever suit and rank their possessor chooses, while other games will specify the suit and rank of the wild cards. Sometimes jokers will be used as wild cards.

Including these cards can mean that two players can hold the same full house, or three of a kind, which in a game with no wild cards, would be impossible. In these instances, the rank of the other cards in the hand will decide the winner.

DEALING

Every game of poker has a dealer, from a Friday night game to the finals of the World Poker Championships. Casinos and organized events or championships employ professional dealers, but the dealer can often be one of the players.

The dealer's job is to police the game. They ensure that each player bets the required amount at the right time. The dealer also announces the winner of each hand... and their word is law!

Where there is no official dealer players take turns to fulfil the role. Since the cards are dealt to the left of the dealer and the person sitting on the left is the first player to bet, games with a professional dealer use a "dealer's button" to indicate

who has the nominal role of dealer in each round.

Casinos don't make money from poker in the same way as they do from roulette or blackjack. The dealer will be paid for by the players in the form of either a levy on each round's winnings or an agreed hourly fee per person.

ETIQUETTE

Don't bet out of sequence. It will only slow the game down as well as marking you out as the novice at the table—which is never a good idea!

HOUSE RULES

Although individual poker games have rules, there are many other rules of play that will need to be agreed among all of the players before the first hand is dealt. This will help prevent any misunderstandings and will allow the game to flow easily. Many of these rules are the responsibility of the dealer to enforce.

1. Agree an initial buy-in amount so that all players have the same amount of money. This will mean that no one player has an initial financial advantage.

2. Play with chips of different colors representing different values instead of cash. This will stop players digging into their wallets if they fall short. It is also a good way to stop people betting beyond what they can afford.

3. Set a limit for the ante, minimum bets and raises.

4. Set a maximum number of raises per betting round.

5. Will there be any variations to the standard rules of the game—will it be played as lowball (page 32) or are you going to use any wild cards?

6. If the dealer is also a player, the deal should rotate so that each player has an equal number of turns dealing.

7. Play is started by the person to the left of the dealer and rotates clockwise in turn.

8. If two players have the same winning hand, they split the pot.

9. At the showdown the person who raised or bet last shows their hand first. Players then reveal their cards in turn clockwise around the table. If there is only one player remaining they do not have to reveal their hand.

10. Never show your hand to another player and be careful not to reveal any cards when folding—you don't want to give active players a clue to what cards may still be in play.

HAND RANKS

The hands of poker are ranked as follows from the highest to the lowest. If there is a situation where two players have the same hand, the winner is the player holding the highest card.

FIVE OF A KIND

A five of a kind is only possible when using multiple decks, wild cards or jokers, and is the highest possible hand. This is a hand with the same number from each of the four suits, plus a joker or wild card. In the unlikely event that more than one player has five of a kind, the higher numbered cards win.

ROYAL FLUSH

An ace-high straight flush is called a
royal flush, and is the highest
natural hand. The chances of being
dealt a royal flush are 650,000-1
and a straight flush 72,200-1.

STRAIGHT FLUSH

A straight flush is when a hand has
five sequential cards all of the same
suit (such as 6-7-8-9-10 of clubs).
As well as appearing in a royal flush
an ace can also be used in a low
straight (A-2-3-4-5). A straight may
not "wrap around," as in Q-K-A-2-3.

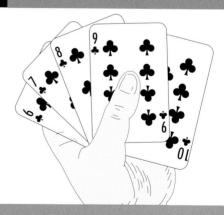

FOUR OF A KIND

Four of a kind is simply four cards of the same rank. If there are two or more hands that qualify, the hand with the highest-ranked cards wins. This could only ever happen in a game with many wild cards. The chances of being dealt four of a kind are 4,200-1.

FULL HOUSE

A full house is three of a kind plus a pair (such as Q-Q-Q-4-4). If more than one hand holds a full house, the hand with the highest three of a kind wins. So Q-Q-Q-4-4 beats J-J-J-A-A, which beats J-J-J-Q-Q. Two players can only hold an identical full house when playing with two decks or using wild cards. The chances of being dealt a full house are 700-1.

FLUSH

A flush is a non-sequential hand where all of the cards are the same suit, such as K-9-7-4-3, all of hearts. When flushes tie, follow the rules for high card. The chances of being dealt a flush are 510-1.

STRAIGHT

A straight is five cards of any suit running concurrently, such as 6-7-8-9-10. An ace may either be high (10-J-Q-K-A) or low (A-2-3-4-5). As with a straight flush, a straight may not wrap around. When straights tie, the highest straight wins (A-K-Q-J-10 beats K-Q-J-10-9, which in turn would beat 5-4-3-2-A). If two straights have the same value, they split the pot. The chances of being dealt a straight are 250-1.

THREE OF A KIND

This is three cards of the same rank, with the two other cards in the hand not matching; otherwise it would be a full house. Again, in a tie situation, the highest three of a kind wins. If both are the same rank (only possible if playing with multiple decks or wild cards), then compare the high card. The chances of being dealt a three of a kind are 48-1.

TWO PAIR

This is a hand with two different pairs and a fifth card. The highest pair wins ties. If both hands have the same high pair, the highest second pair wins. If both hands have the same pairs, the highest fifth card wins. The chances of being dealt two pair are 21-1.

PAIR

One pair with three other different cards. Highest pair wins, and then the highest card breaks ties. The chances of being dealt a pair are 12-5.

HIGH CARD

This is any hand which does not contain any of the above hands. If no player has a pair or better, then the highest card wins. If several players tie for the highest card, look at the second highest, then the third highest, and so on. High card is also used to break ties when several hands have the same type of hand (pair, flush, straight etc). Aces are normally high in tie break situations unless declared otherwise at the start of the game. The odds of not being dealt a pair are 2-1.

ODDS AND PROBABILITIES

Like many things in life, winning at poker relies on skill, luck, and the probability of a situation even occurring.

As poker is a betting game it is a good idea to keep the odds in mind when you are deciding whether or not to pursue a hand. There are three different kinds of odds to consider. Of course, there are the card odds, which will reveal the probability of being dealt particular hands, or developing a particular hand during the course of the game.

Then there are the investment odds, which look at whether or not, based on your hand, it is a good risk for the amount of money you stand to win when considered against the money you must outlay. The final odds are the edge odds, where you need to assess the other players, and their ability.

There are 2,598,960 possible poker hands in a 52-card deck. The table opposite shows the number of possible combinations as well as the odds of being dealt one of these in an original five-card hand.

TABLE OF ODDS

Hand	Number of combinations	Odds of being dealt
Royal Flush	4	650,000-1
Straight Flush	36	72,200-1
Four of a Kind	624	4200-1
Full House	3,744	700-1
Flush	5,108	510-1
Straight	10,200	250-1
Three of a Kind	54,912	48-1
Two Pair	123,552	21-1
One Pair	1,098,240	12-5
No Pair	1,302,540	2-1

ASSESSING THE RISKS

Bearing these odds in mind, there are already some things that can be inferred:

- The more players, the greater the chance of there being a high-ranking hand. Likewise, the more players, the less the value of a lower-ranked hand.
- If you don't have at least a pair, or four cards needed for a flush or straight, fold.
- The chance of improving your hand enough to beat all the other players if you have been dealt a bad hand is remote.
- Accept that unless you are really lucky, you will fold most of the time in the first round.

Having studied the odds of each hand you will quickly realize that the image of high dealing hands shown in the movies is obviously false. Most poker games come down to careful strategies and balancing the odds, not betting everything on a million-to-one shot

QUOTES AND QUIPS

"Whether he likes it or not, a man's character is stripped bare at the poker table; if the other poker players read him better than he does, he has only himself to blame. Unless he is both able and prepared to see himself as others do, flaws and all, he will be a loser in poker, as in life."

Anthony Holden

LOW POKER

Low poker or lowball is a common variation that is used when playing many popular games—in low poker the order of the winning hands can change.

In this variation, it is the player with the lowest hand that wins.

There may be some changes to the hand ranks, although these are not universal so should be confirmed between players before the game begins.

The most common rules are:

1. Aces are always low, ranked below the twos.

2. Straights and flushes are not recognized hand ranks.

3. A hand is always counted as the highest rank possible. For example, Q-Q-Q-2-2 would be a full house and not a pair of twos.

Within these rules, this means that the best hand would be 5-4-3-2-A, because this would not count as a straight.

BETTING

Poker is essentially a gambling game. You are betting that you will have a higher hand than any other player left in the game.

If you are playing with friends, or in a club, it is a good idea to set betting limits up front. This will stop the game from getting out of hand, and people losing more money than they can afford. Among friends, lower limits are usually set for the ante and raising. It is not worth losing a friend over a game of cards! Casino games are different. All bets must be honored and once you lose you must pay.

BETTING IN A CASINO

Casino tables all have betting limits designed to stop inexperienced players from losing too heavily. Casino tables also feature table stakes. This means that you can only bet using the money you have on the table at the start of each round, you can't go back to your wallet for more stake money, no matter how good your hand is!

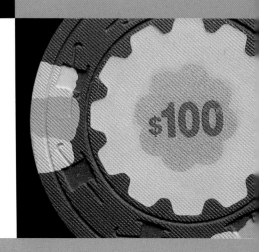

POKER CHIPS

In a casino large piles of money just lying around on tables would be a big security risk so they keep all the money in one safe place, the strongroom. When you arrive at the casino you exchange your betting money for chips. Chips come in a range of color-coded values to reflect the stakes being played for, from a single dollar to many thousands. At home you could easily assign your own values to the different colored chips, or just play with good old cash.

UPPING THE ANTE

In most games you must ante an amount just to have cards dealt to you. The ante is like a fee for playing, and is put in the center of the table as the pot. From here on, players will bet into the pot in the middle based on how good they think their hand is. During this time if a player doubts that their hand will win they will fold. At the end of the game, the player with the highest hand, or most convincing bluff, who didn't fold, wins the pot.

Betting will normally move in a clockwise direction. The number of rounds of betting is determined by the rules of each game. Often these will be announced by the dealer before any cards are dealt.

CALL

When you call, you are betting enough to keep you in the game. This bet will match what the stakes have been raised to since the last time you bet. For example, if your first bet was $1 and now the bet is $3, you will owe the pot $2.

RAISE

When you raise, you first need to bet enough to match what has been wagered since your last go (as in calling or seeing), then you raise the bet a further amount. It is up to you how much you raise the stakes but a limit is normally set before the game begins.

Continuing the example above, if you had bet $1, the other player raised you $2 (up to $3), then you might raise another $3 (up to $6). This would mean that you would pay $5 to the pot ($2 for calling and $3 for your raise).

FOLD

If you do not believe that you have a strong hand, or could not bluff your way through the game, you can fold. This means that you do not pay any more money to the pot, but you also cannot win any money. You can fold when it is your turn during any round. Sometimes it is just best to get out!

Betting continues until everyone calls or folds after a raise or initial bet.

STRATEGIES

When it comes to developing your strategy for playing poker, there are many things to consider. Not only do you need to know the table or house rules, but you need to have your own set of guiding principles.

When starting out, here are some points that you should consider:

- Don't start a game without enough money. Thirty to forty times the table limit is a good guide.

- Never bet more than you can afford. Set yourself a limit and stick to it.

- If you have a good hand, make others pay to see it.

- If you are dealt a bad hand, get out! The odds of improving a bad hand enough to win are slim. Remember there are no prizes for second place!

- During the game, if you feel you are beaten, fold. Don't waste good money on bad cards!

- Don't think that you can beat a more skilled player. You may win a little, but you can also lose a lot!

- Remember it is only a game. Winning a pot is not worth losing friends over!

- The object of the game is to beat the other players to win the pot, not to have the highest hand. Remember, if everyone else folds, you win the lot!

MORE STRATEGIES

Once you have played a few games, the following strategic
thoughts might help you to understand the psychology of the
game, and the people who play it!

SENSIBLE BETTING

There is no point in putting money into a pot to see what is going to happen, you just end up losing more money than necessary. Likewise, if you scare other players into folding with a big raise when you are chasing the pot, you will win less money than you could have.

Gradual raises over several rounds will maximize your winnings if you have a good hand.

Remember to set yourself a limit and stick to it. Never bet more money than you can afford to lose!

DO YOUR SUMS

Look at how much money you stand to win, in relation to how much money you need to outlay when you are deciding whether to call or bet.

PLAYING PATTERNS

Look for patterns in how your opponents play, and assess any areas of weakness. Do they either call or raise on mediocre to good hands? Is there a player that will never raise regardless of their hand? Does anyone fold on anything less than a high three of a kind?

ADJUST YOUR PLAY

Once you understand the other players' styles you can adjust yours accordingly. If you come up against a player who constantly bluffs, then when you do get a high hand, there is a chance to call their bluff.

TELLING SIGNS

Be aware of your reaction to your cards and that of others. Does your hand shake when you are bluffing? Can your friend not look you in the eye when they have a high hand? These telling signs can give the game away.

BLUFF AWAY

Use bluffing in moderation, but do use it! This is an essential part of the game of poker and could win you money. The player who sits back waiting for a good hand to collect a pot, will lose more hands than they win.

DRAW GAMES

In this style of game players receive all of their cards in the
initial deal, and then have the option to exchange some
in subsequent rounds.

FIVE-CARD DRAW

Players	*3-7*
Cards	*A standard 52-card deck*
Initial deal	*Five cards to each player, face down*
Winner	*Highest hand*

Five-card draw is one of the most common types of poker, and is probably the
best game to start with to learn the basics. Players are dealt five cards each face
down, starting with the player to the left of the dealer. Players then look at their
cards and as their turn comes they will either bet or fold. When folding, never
show your cards to anyone.

Once all bets are placed, players may then exchange any number of cards with
the dealer. For example, if you have a pair of kings, you may discard three cards
and receive three new cards from the remaining deck. This is known as the draw.

Once every player has completed the draw or stuck with their original cards, a
second round of betting will take place, where each player can fold, call or raise.

The third and final round of betting is over when everyone is square with the pot! Once all bets are completed, there is a showdown where all remaining players reveal their hands. The winner is the player with the highest-ranking hand. If only one player remains at the end of the second betting round, there is no showdown and the player wins the pot without having to expose their cards.

Variations

Wild card—Adding wild cards to play, and five of a kind.

High/low—The highest hand and lowest hand split the pot.

Lowball—Lowest hand wins (see page 32).

Limited exchange—Allowing only up to three cards to be exchanged. Four cards can be drawn if the player reveals the fifth to be an ace.

Double draw—After the first exchange and subsequent betting, there is another exchange and betting round.

THREE-LEGGED RACE

Players	3-8
Cards	A standard 52-card deck
Initial deal	Five cards to each player, face down
Winner	Highest and lowest hands

This is known as a triple-legged game, which means that the first player to win three legs gets the pot.

At the end of each game, one leg is won by the player with the highest hand (played as five-card draw), and another leg is also awarded to the player with the lowest hand.

If more than one player wins their third leg in the same hand, the pot is split.

CHEAT!

Yes, some people do cheat at poker. There are many ways to cheat, including marking the cards beforehand or during play by "thumbnailing" or crimping. Players may "mistakenly" call a straight as straight flush to scoop the pot. Dextrous players may use sleight of hand to palm cards or otherwise manipulate the deck, while others simply steal from the pot while no-one is looking. Check if your fellow gamers are exchanging signs. Are two or more players colluding?

SIX BACK TO FIVE

Players	*3-8*
Cards	*A standard 52-card deck*
Initial deal	*Six cards to each player, face down*
Winner	*Highest hand*

All the players ante up. Six cards are dealt face down to each player. The game then follows the same rules as a regular five-card draw game. The only difference is that each player draws one less card than they discard. This means that if a player wants two new cards, they will have to discard three cards from their hand.

Therefore, because each player draws one less card than they receive, each player ends up with a five-card hand. Once the first betting round has taken place and players have drawn and discarded their hands, a final betting round ensues and the best five-card hand wins.

ALL FOR ONE OR ONE FOR ALL

Players	*3-8*
Cards	*A standard 52-card deck*
Initial deal	*Five cards to each player, face down*
Winner	*Highest hand*

All the players ante up. Five cards are dealt face down to each player. After the initial betting round, each player can discard either one or all of their cards in their hand for an equal number of replacements from the deck.

The game continues with more rounds of betting and drawing where again players may change one or all five of their cards. This continues until there are fewer cards in the deck than players left in the game. The showdown follows, where the highest hand wins.

POKER TRIVIA
The "Dead Man's Hand" is aces and eights—supposedly held by Wild Bill Hickock when he was gunned down in a saloon in Deadwood, South Dakota.

ANACONDA

Players	*4-7*
Cards	*A standard 52-card deck*
Initial deal	*Seven cards to each player, face down*
Winner	*Highest hand*

Seven cards are dealt face down to each player who antes up. A round of betting takes place, then each player passes three cards that they want to discard from their hand to the player on their left. In turn, you will receive three cards from the player on your right. After a second betting round, everyone passes two cards to the player on their left and receives the same from the right.

After another betting round, players then pass just one card to their left. Each player then discards two cards, keeping their best five-card hand.

Players then arrange their remaining five cards into the order that they want to reveal them to the table, with the card they want to show first on top.

They are then placed in a stack face down on the table. You must be certain you have them in the order you like, because they cannot be rearranged later.

On the dealer's instruction, each player flips their first card. A round of betting takes place starting with the player with the highest card. The cards are now revealed one by one, with a betting round following each card until all of the cards are revealed.

Pay close attention to opponents' hands as they are revealed—you could work out after the second card that they have a higher hand than you and save yourself some money for the next game. As usual, the highest-ranking hand revealed wins the pot.

ASSASSIN

Players	*3-7*
Cards	*A standard 52-card deck, plus a joker*
Initial deal	*A blind card, plus four held cards face down to each player*
Winner	*Highest hand*

All the players ante up. Four cards are dealt face down on top of a blind card dealt to each player. Players may look at their four-card hand, but not their blind card. Players place their bets and then there is a draw where they can exchange up to two cards. A second round of betting or folding follows.

The remaining players must now flip their blind card for all to see. If a player's blind card is the joker they have been "assassinated," and are out of the game—but they must first match the amount of money in the pot. All players who do not hold the joker as the blind card, leave their card face up on the table. This will be included as the fifth card in their final hand. Play continues with a third and final betting round and a showdown. Best hand wins the pot. If the joker is held in a player's hand, it is a wild card.

FRUSTRATION

Players	*3 or more*
Cards	*A standard 52-card deck*
Initial deal	*Two cards to each player, face down*
Winner	*Highest hand*

This is basically two-card draw poker. Two cards are dealt to each player followed by a betting round and then a draw, where both cards can be exchanged. There is then a final betting round (unless it is agreed that there will be another draw). Each hand will have either a pair or a high card. Highest hand wins. Any ties are resolved by taking the suit rankings of each hand into consideration (see page 72).

(see page 72)

QUOTES AND QUIPS

"Poker is the game closest to the western conception of life, where life and thought are recognized as intimately combined, where free will prevails over philosophies of fate or of chance, where men are considered moral agents and where—at least in the short run—the important thing is not what happens but what people think happens."

Charles Lamb

JACKS OR BETTER, TRIPS TO WIN

Players	*3-7*
Cards	*A standard 52-card deck*
Initial deal	*Five cards face down to each player*
Winner	*Highest hand*

Each anted up player is dealt a hand of five cards. The initial betting round can only be opened by a player holding a pair of jacks or higher. If nobody can open the betting, then each player antes again and the cards are re-dealt by the player on the dealer's left. If a player is able to open the betting, the game is played like five-card draw until the showdown. Then, anyone with three of a kind, or better, must reveal their hand, highest wins. If nobody has a hand to show—that is nobody has at least three of a kind—the hands are folded and a new round begins. The pot remains for the next hand.

Variations

If no player can open with a pair of jacks or better, then the game can be played as lowball (see page 32), with a draw and final betting round.

Another variation is if nobody has a hand to show, everyone still in play may make another exchange. Repeat the steps of the game until someone wins.

PSYCHO

Players	3-6
Cards	*A standard 52-card deck*
Initial deal	*Five cards to each player, face down*
Winner	*Highest and lowest hands*

The game begins as regular five-card draw. After the first draw, each player reveals three cards from their hand face up on the table. The player with the best hand showing starts the second round of betting.

Each player is now dealt another card face up. Again the player with the best hand showing opens a third betting round. Each player is now dealt a final card face down which is included in their hand. Everyone will now have seven cards, three in their hand plus four face up.

The player with the best hand showing opens the final betting round, and this is followed by the showdown, where five-card hands are created from all seven cards. The pot is split equally between the players with the highest and lowest hands.

SPIT IN THE OCEAN

Players	*3-8*
Cards	*A standard 52-card deck*
Initial deal	*Four cards face down to each player, one card up in the middle.*
Winner	*Highest hand*

Each player is dealt four cards, then one card is placed in the center of the table face up. This card plays as if it were the fifth card in every player's hand. This card, along with all other cards of the same rank, is wild. For example, if a player held Q-Q-4-6, and the card in the center was also a six, then the hand could be a four of a kind (Q-Q-Q-Q-4) because the sixes would take on whichever rank the player wished.

The game is played like five-card draw. The first betting round is played, followed by a draw in which each player replaces cards from his poker hand with an equal number, so that each player still has only four cards in their hand. A final betting round is followed by a showdown. The highest hand wins.

THREES

Players	*3-10*
Cards	*A standard 52-card deck*
Initial deal	*Five cards to each player, face down*
Winner	*Highest hand*

Five cards are dealt face down to each player. After checking their cards and an initial betting round, each player can freely exchange cards with any other player (suits and values are not revealed). You can change as many cards with as many players as you wish, but you must always exchange the same number of cards, so that all players retain a five-card hand.

There will be lots of shouts of "Does anyone want to swap two cards?" When all trading is done, there is a final betting round followed by the showdown. Highest hand wins.

ETIQUETTE

It is considered rude to throw your bet into the pot as it makes it hard for the other players to see how much you are betting. All bets should be stacked neatly in front of each player.

WHISKEY POKER

Players	3-7
Cards	A standard 52-card deck
Initial deal	Five cards to each player, face down, plus five face up in the center
Winner	Highest hand

Five cards are dealt to each player face down, and an extra five-card hand is dealt face up as a kitty. An initial betting round takes place. Beginning with the player to the left of the dealer and continuing clockwise in turn, each has the option to exchange all or part of their hand with the kitty, or keep their dealt hand. If a player chooses to take the kitty, they will then put their dealt hand in the center face up. If no player decides to take the kitty, it is then turned face down.

Beginning on the left of the player who took the kitty (or the player to the left of the dealer if no one did), each player may draw as many cards as they like from the kitty and replace them with cards from their hand. These new cards are placed face up so that all players have a kitty of five cards to select from and every player always has five cards.

This continues round the table with each player either exchanging or knocking on the table to signify that they will not be exchanging. Once a player has knocked, it means that each of the other players has only one more chance to exchange with the kitty. Once play reaches the player to the right of the player who knocked, there is a final betting round and a showdown, where the highest hands wins.

If none of the players knock in the first round they all have another opportunity to exchange cards until one of them knocks.

STUD GAMES

In stud poker games players receive a mix of cards face up, and others face down, dealt in multiple betting rounds. The face-down cards (hole cards), are only for the eyes of the recipient, however the face-up cards (door cards) are for all the players to view.

Stud poker is normally played with hands of either five or seven cards. A seven-card hand will end up with three cards face down and four face up, and a five-card hand will have one card face down and four face up.

SEVEN-CARD STUD

Players	3-7
Cards	A standard 52-card deck
Initial deal	Two cards face down (hole cards), plus one face up (door card)
Winner	Highest five-card hand, out of seven cards

Players must ante into the pot to receive their initial cards; two face down, plus one face up. There are five betting rounds, not including the ante. The first betting round is initiated by the player with the lowest face-up card by suit. Suits are ranked: spades (highest), hearts, diamonds and, lastly, clubs. On subsequent rounds, the player with the highest door card starts betting. If hands are tied, the player nearest to the left of the dealer acts first.

Betting Limits

There are two betting limits set; usually the higher is double the lower limit. Each bet and raise during the first two rounds of betting is set at the lower limit.

In a game with limits of $1 and $2, the first two rounds will be $1 betting. However, if a player has a pair in their two face-up cards, all players have the option to bet either the lower or higher limit. Once a player bets the higher limit, all subsequent raises must be made at that limit. All bets and raises during the last three rounds are set at the higher limit.

The players, in turn, must call, raise or fold. Each player is then dealt a second face-up card. There are two more betting rounds and deals of face up cards.

Then, the fourth round of betting, each player is dealt their last card face down. After a fifth and final betting round there is a showdown.

Players may use any five of their seven cards to make their best hand. Highest hand wins. Suits are not used in determining the winner and tied hands split the pot.

FIVE-CARD STUD

Players	*3-10*
Cards	*A standard 52-card deck*
Initial deal	*One card face down (hole card), plus one face up (door card)*
Winner	*Highest five-card hand*

All players place an ante. Players are each dealt two cards; one face up and the other face down. The player with the lowest-ranked door card must place the opening bet. Working clockwise from the dealer, each player must either call, raise or fold.

Each of the remaining players is then dealt another card face up, followed by another round of betting. After the third card is dealt, the betting is always started by the player with the highest-ranked poker hand showing.

This process continues until all players have been dealt five cards, one face down, and four face up, or until only one player remains. All those still in play reveal their fifth card and the highest hand wins.

SEVENS TAKE ALL

Sevens take all is a variation that can be used in conjunction with many other house rules, and added to any stud game.

Basically, a pair of sevens is the best hand a player can hold. If a player is dealt a seven face up, this can lead to angst at the table because the other players will not know if they have another seven face down.

Lots of bluffing and high bets can make this an interesting variation. If two players have a pair of sevens, the highest-ranking card of the remaining three cards determines the winner.

QUOTES AND QUIPS

"In poker there is, of course, no attempt to disguise the aggressive element. Poker is a fighting game, a game in which each player tries to get the better of every other player and does so by fair means or foul so long as he obeys the rules of the game. He may bluff or lie about his own strength, the object of the game being either to frighten the other players into believing that he has greater strength or else to prove it."

Karl Meninger

AUCTION

Players	*3-7*
Cards	*A standard 52-card deck*
Initial deal	*Two cards face down (hole cards) to each player, plus one face up (door card) dealt to the table*
Winner	*Highest five-card hand, out of seven cards*

Often played as a variation of seven-card stud, players are initially dealt two cards face down, plus a single card is dealt face up in the middle of the table.

Each person then secretly chooses an amount, of at least the minimum bet, and conceals it in their hand. Then everyone reveals their bets at once. The person who bids highest, puts their bid in the pot and can either keep the auction card or designate it to another player.

If more than one player bets the same, the bidder nearest the dealer, rotating clockwise, selects next. All bids are added to the pot. Play continues in the same way until all players have seven cards, then comes the showdown. Highest five-card hand wins.

CHOOSE YOUR OWN

Players   3-7

Cards   *A standard 52-card deck*

Initial deal   *Two cards face down and one card face up to each player*

Winner   *Highest hand*

After the ante is paid, two cards are dealt face down plus one card face up to each player. After a round of betting one card is dealt face up in the middle for each player. So, if there are four players, there will be four cards dealt.

The player with the lowest face-up card gets to pick which card they want for their hand. The player with the second-lowest goes next. This continues until all the cards in the middle are taken. If two players tie, the closest of the two to the dealer's left goes first. Another round of betting is followed by another round of face-up cards, with the lowest hand choosing first again. Follow this format for one more round so that each player has six cards. After a betting round, everyone is dealt their seventh card face down. A final betting round follows and then there is a showdown. The player with the highest five-card hand wins.

Variation
This can also be played as a five-card hand.

HAVE A HEART

Players	3-7
Cards	A standard 52-card deck
Initial deal	Two cards face down, plus one face up to each player
Winner	Highest hand

This game follows the format of seven-card stud. However, in this variation, when a heart is dealt face up, that player may take a card from another player. They can select a card that is either face up or face down. The player whose card is taken does not draw a replacement, so will only have six cards from which to select their five-card showdown hand. In the same way, the player with the heart has eight cards to choose from. The highest five-card hand wins.

Variation
The player who is dealt any heart can trade a card for one from any other player at the table. This may be either a face-up or a face-down card. The rule applies whenever a heart is dealt.

HENWAY

Players	3-5
Cards	A standard 52-card deck
Initial deal	Ten cards face down to each player
Winner	Highest and lowest hands

Ten cards are dealt face down to each player. Each player then looks at their hand and splits their ten cards into two five-card hands. These are then laid face down on the table in two stacks, in order of how the player wants to reveal them. There is a betting round before a card from each pile is flipped, until all of the cards are revealed. The start of the betting is rotated around the table. As each card is revealed players may fold either or both hands if they feel things are not going their way. Highest and lowest hands split the pot. A player with both the highest and the lowest hands takes it all!

ROLL YOUR OWN

Players   3-7

Cards   A standard 52-card deck

Initial deal Three cards face down (hole cards)

Winner   Best five-card hand, out of seven cards

This variation of seven-card stud allows each player to select which cards will be face up for the other players to see, while still maintaining the three-down, four-up format.

Each player is dealt three cards face down, then, on the count of three, chooses one of their three to turn face up. This is followed by a betting round, started by the player with the highest card showing.

The fourth card is dealt face down, and again each player must turn one of their cards over. This format continues until each player has been dealt six cards, and there have been four betting rounds. At this point, each player will have four cards face up, and two face down. The final card is dealt face down and then there is a final betting round. A showdown follows and the highest hand wins.

SPANISH STUD

Players	*Up to six players if using one deck. (Four players for seven-card stud)*
Cards	*Deck with all the twos, threes, fours, fives, and sixes (twenty cards) removed*
Initial deal	*Either one card up and one down to each player for Spanish five-card stud or two up and two down for Spanish seven-card stud*
Winner	*Best five-card (or seven card) hand*

This popular variation on five- or seven-card stud is played with a reduced deck. By taking out the lower numbered cards the chances of holding a high hand are increased. As there are only 32 cards in the deck the number of players is also limited. The structure of the game follows the standard five- or seven-card stud versions (page 74 and 72).

Variation
The number of players can be increased by using two (or more) decks of cards.

THE GOOD, THE BAD AND THE UGLY

Players	3-7
Cards	A standard 52-card deck
Initial deal	Two cards face down (hole cards), plus one face up (door card) to each player, and three cards face down to the table.
Winner	Highest five-card hand, out of seven cards

This game is basically seven-card stud but with a twist. Players ante up and, along with the two cards face down, and the one face up dealt to each player, an additional three cards are dealt face down on the table. A betting round follows and a fourth card is dealt face up, while the first of the cards in the center of the table is flipped, this is the "Good." All cards of the same rank are considered wild.

Another betting round and the fifth card is dealt, the second center card is flipped and this is the "Bad." All cards of the same rank in players' hands must be discarded from play. Finally, after the last betting round the sixth card is dealt, and the last remaining table card is flipped the "Ugly." Anyone with a face-up card of the same rank must fold. A showdown follows and the highest hand wins.

SHARED GAMES

Community, or shared, poker games are distinguished by the fact that a mixture of cards are dealt to each player, as well as to the table. Betting rounds often take place between the table cards being flipped. The table cards can be used by each player to help them make the best possible hand.

TEXAS HOLD 'EM

Players	*3-20*
Cards	*A standard 52-card deck*
Initial deal	*Two cards face down to each player*
Winner	*Highest hand*

Texas hold 'em uses a disc called a dealer button (which you can improvise at home) to indicate who is the dealer, and blind bets instead of antes. Before the cards are dealt, the two players to the left of the button must place live bets called the small and large blinds. They are blind bets because the players have not yet seen any cards, and live, because they count towards any further bets in the first betting round. Before the game starts, the players should decide the amount for the small blind, then the large blind is usually twice that.

To begin, two cards are dealt face down to each player. Then betting continues clockwise, starting with the player to the left of those who placed the blind bets.

Each player must bet, call, raise, or fold. The player who placed the large blind bet has the advantage of going last and can call or raise.

Three community cards are then dealt face up in the center of the table and another betting round takes place, beginning with the player to the left of the dealer button. Then another card is dealt face up, followed by another round of betting.

The fifth and final card is dealt face up and the last round of betting takes place. During the showdown, players may use any combination of their own cards and the community cards to make their best five-card hand. Highest hand wins.

CINCINNATI

Players	*3-9*
Cards	*A standard 52-card deck*
Initial deal	*Five cards face down to each player, plus five cards face down to the table*
Winner	*Highest hand*

Five cards are dealt face down to each player, followed by five cards laid out face down in the center of the table.

The center cards are flipped one at a time, with a round of betting between each one being revealed. Repeat this format until all of the cards are flipped. A showdown follows the last betting round. Each player will make their best five-card hand using a combination of their own cards and the community cards. Highest hand wins.

H-BOMB

Players	*3-7*
Cards	*A standard 52-card deck*
Initial deal	*Four cards face down to each player, plus seven cards in shape of an 'H'*
Winner	*Highest hand*

Each player is dealt four cards face down. The dealer then places seven cards face-down in an H-shape, three in two parallel columns and then one in the middle to join the second row. The dealer now chooses a card on the "H" to flip face up, and this is followed by a betting round.

The remainder of the community cards are flipped one at a time, as the dealer chooses, with a betting round between each flip. Once all seven cards are revealed there is a final betting round.

For the showdown, players must use the cards from their hand, plus one of the five rows of three cards (two vertical, two diagonal and one horizontal) created by the "H," to make their best five-card hand. Highest hand wins.

OHIO

Players	3-9
Cards	A standard 52-card deck
Initial deal	Five cards face down to each player plus five cards face down to the table
Winner	Highest hand

Five cards are dealt face down to each player, followed by five cards laid out face down in the center of the table. The game is played similarly to Cincinnati (page 94) with the center cards being flipped one at a time, with a round of betting between each one. This is repeated until all of the cards are flipped. Once all of the community cards are revealed, the lowest-ranking card is declared wild. Any other cards on the table and in players' hands of the same rank therefore become wild also.

A showdown follows the last betting round. Each player will make their best five-card hand using any of their own cards plus any of the community cards. Highest hand wins.

OMAHA HOLD 'EM

Players	*3-11*
Cards	*A standard 52-card deck*
Initial deal	*Four cards face down to each player*
Winner	*Highest hand*

Omaha is based on Texas hold 'em (page 92) but brings a few variables to the table.

This is a nine-card poker game consisting of four cards for each player plus five community cards. Play begins with the four cards being dealt to each player face down. Blinds are placed, and the dealer button is used in the same way as with Texas hold 'em. The betting round continues, with each player deciding either to bet, call, raise or fold in turn.

The five community cards are then dealt to the center of the table face down. Three cards are then turned face up, followed by a betting round. A round of betting also follows as the final two cards are turned.

After the final betting round all players remaining in the hand will then show all of their cards. Players must use two cards from their own hand combined with three community cards to make their best five-card poker hand.

OUT AT HOME

Players	*3-11*
Cards	*A standard 52-card deck*
Initial deal	*Three cards face down to each player, plus four cards face down in a diamond formation (community cards)*
Winner	*Highest hand*

An ante is paid to the pot. Players are dealt three cards each face down. Four community cards are then dealt face down in a diamond formation. An initial betting round takes place. Each of the community cards is then flipped face up one at a time, starting with the "first base." A betting round takes place after each card is flipped, ending with the "home plate."

If the last home plate card is a picture card, then the hand is dead, the remaining players that did not fold re-ante, and a new hand is dealt. Threes and nines are wild. If any of the community cards is a four, each remaining player is dealt an extra card. Some games are played so that an extra payment is required to make cards wild—this helps to increase the pot! The highest hand, using the player's own cards and the community cards wins.

TENNESSEE

Players	*3-9*
Cards	*A standard 52-card deck*
Initial deal	*Five cards face down to each player plus four cards face down to the table*
Winner	*Highest hand*

This game is played in a similar format to Cincinnati (page 94), however players can only bet and raise predetermined amounts. The amount for one bet needs to be agreed before the game begins.

Play begins with five cards being dealt face down to each player, followed by four cards laid out face down in the center of the table. The center cards are flipped one at a time, with a round of betting between each one being revealed. Repeat this format until all of the cards are flipped. Then it's showdown. The player with the best five-card hand takes the pot.

In the first betting round, the opening bet can only be one unit and players can only raise two units. When the second card is revealed, players can only bet two units or raise four units. For the third card, betting is three units and raising is six units. Finally, four units is the bet for the fourth card, and eight units the raise.

"It's hard work. Gambling. Playing poker. Don't let anyone tell you different. Think about what it's like sitting at a poker table with people whose only goal is to cut your throat, take your money, and leave you out back talking to yourself about what went wrong inside. That probably sounds harsh. But that's the way it is at the poker table. If you don't believe me, then you're the lamb that's going off to the slaughter."

Stu Unger

TIC TAC TOE

Players	3-11
Cards	A standard 52-card deck
Initial deal	Two cards face down to each player, plus nine cards face up arranged in a three by three grid (community cards)
Winner	Highest hand

Each player antes up then receives three chips or counters plus two cards face down. Nine community cards are then dealt face up in a three by three grid in the center. There is one betting round. After this, each player in turn must announce their best five-card hand using the two cards from their hand plus a row from the community cards. This row must be used in its entirety and may be either horizontal, vertical or diagonal. Once you have announced your hand you cannot change your mind if you happen to see a better one. The highest hand takes the pot and all other players must toss one of their counters into the middle towards the next pot.

All cards are then discarded and a new hand is dealt to all players who still have chips. Play continues in this format until only one player has counters left. Any tied hands are resolved by using the ranking of the different suits (page 72).